Schöningh

D1700836

Discover ...

TOPICS FOR ADVANCED LEARNERS
edited by Engelbert Thaler

Our Environment
A State of Emergency?

by Stephen Speight

Song texts chosen by Karsten Witsch

© 2009 Bildungshaus Schulbuchverlage
Westermann Schroedel Diesterweg Schöningh Winklers GmbH
Braunschweig, Paderborn, Darmstadt

www.schoeningh-schulbuch.de
Schöningh Verlag, Jühenplatz 1–3, 33098 Paderborn

Druck 5 4 3 2 1 / Jahr 2013 12 11 10 09
Die letzte Zahl bezeichnet das Jahr dieses Druckes.

Umschlaggestaltung: Franz-Josef Domke, Hannover
Umschlagabbildung: © vario images
Druck und Bindung: westermann druck GmbH, Braunschweig

ISBN 978-3-14-040108-1

Contents

Getting started

This is an extract from the Journal of Omn, which forms part of a short story by John Wyndham. Omn is an inhabitant of a dying planet who is about to travel to another planet, hoping to start a new and better life there ...

... I have looked again through the telescope at our new home. Our group is, I think, lucky. It is a planet which is neither too young nor too old. Conditions were better than before, with less cloud over its surface. It shines like a blue pearl. Much of the part I saw was covered with water – more than two-thirds of it, they tell me, is under water. It will be good to be in a place where irrigation and water supply are not one of the main problems of life. Nevertheless, one hopes that we will be fortunate enough to make our landing on dry ground, or there may be very great difficulties ...

I am glad that our group is going to the blue, shining world: it seems to beckon us, and I am filled with a hope which helps to quieten my fears of the journey.

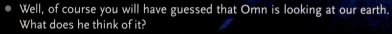

- Well, of course you will have guessed that Omn is looking at our earth. What does he think of it?
- There is an English saying which goes: "Distance lends enchantment to the view." How could this saying apply to the text in the early 21st century (the story was written in the 1950s)? Can anything unpleasant be seen from space?
- Which fairly recent environmental problem in parts of our world is one of the main problems on Omn's planet? Why doesn't he think it can be a problem on our planet? Why is he wrong?

The blue planet

About the Chapter Headings

It's almost impossible to deal with one aspect of the environment without other aspects getting involved. Have a look at the strip cartoon below.

Calvin and Hobbes

Activities

One thing leads to another

1. What is Calvin worried about?

2. Why wasn't he worried before?

Basics

3. How does Calvin explain the greenhouse effect?

4. What aspects of global warming does he mention?

5. Is there anything he hasn't considered?

Calvin – and us?

6. How has his attitude to the environment been inconsistent – until now?

Different sides of the same coin?

The following photos show how difficult it is to keep different aspects of the environment separate.

Cheap flights

Energy shortages

Global warming

Rising sea levels

Desertification

Activities

1. How far do you accept the links implied by the arrows?

2. Is anything important missing?

3. The earth has been warmer than this before – and colder, of course. Maybe a bit of global warming could be a good thing. What do you think?

Disturbing pictures

Does it really matter?

Lucky Earthlings?

There may well be other planets which are as fortunate as ours, but none of them are very near, even in light-year terms. In this book we will be looking at some of the reasons for regarding our planet as a pleasant place to live, some of the ways in which we seem to be intent on trashing it, and some of the ways we may be able to save it. Here are some points which we hope will put you in the right frame of mind for what follows:

➤ Our planet has been **able to support life in one form or another continuously for several hundred million years**. OK, the dinosaurs failed to survive a major upset – perhaps you know something about that – but life still went on and continued to evolve.

Arctic landscape

Melting glaciers in Alaska

➤ Large areas of our planet are in the so-called **Goldilocks zone**. This refers to a well-known fairy story in which Goldilocks wanders into the home of three bears who have gone out for a walk while their porridge cools. She tries out things belonging to father, mother and baby bear, finding one of the three items 'just right' in each case. There are various versions of the story. For example, one of the three plates of porridge is too hot, one is too cold, and one is just right, so of course she eats all the porridge on that plate. As this story is better-known in Britain and the US than in Germany, you may want to check the details on Wikipedia. The fact that our planet has large temperate areas is just as important as the fact that it has a fairly stable history. We probably take this too much for granted. Just think how hot – or cold – conditions are even on other planets in our own solar system. And we have a nice, breathable atmosphere surrounding our beautiful, temperate planet. For now ...

➤ We are living during an **interglacial** period. At one time people believed there had been one ice age which had come to an end. Now we know that there have been several ice ages, with the ice advancing and retreating, sometimes very slowly, sometimes with surprising speed. According to a Scandinavian folk belief, the ice can return permanently if there is 'a summer when the snow does not melt'. On the other hand, we know that the ice can also begin to melt very fast ...

➤ No one would claim that climatic change in the past was our fault. Not everyone thinks that **global warming** is our fault even now, but the consensus of opinion is a) that it *is* our fault, and b) if we don't do something about it soon the consequences will be catastrophic. Some scientists think it is already too late to reverse the trend.

➤ The term **spaceship earth** describes our planet rather well. It implies that mankind has to survive indefinitely on the resources we've got with us here on earth, and that if we wreck the place, there's nowhere else to go.

➤ The conventional wisdom is that the climate was 'just right' in the fairly recent past. Not everyone would agree!

Mountain bikers in Italy

Traffic jam in Peking

Activities

1. Comment on the photographs above, with special reference to their environmental implications.

   Photos

2. Which American politician has won the Nobel Peace Prize for his environmental activities?

   Just a short quiz

3. How do we know that countries like Denmark were once covered with ice?

4. What probably happened to the dinosaurs?

5. What is a carbon footprint?

6. Roughly what proportion of our energy comes from renewable resources?

7. What are greenhouse gases? What is their effect?

8. What do Kyoto and Bali have to do with environmental issues?

9. Who might think that a bit of global warming is a good thing? Would they be right?

Land – Use It, Abuse It, Lose It

About one third of our planet is land – and it's the part we have to live on, grow crops on – and the part where there are still huge rain forests in places where the climate is right. It's also the part where we build houses and factories, dig for minerals – sometime just below the surface – dispose of our rubbish and replace plant life which doesn't make a short-term profit with plant life which does. As a result of our activities we are reducing the amount of land available, and making some of it too dry to be any good to us. However, the inhabitants of Greenland may not be too bothered!

Activities

Do we need them?

1. Why are the rain forests important? After all, England cut down most of its trees to build ships, and the country doesn't seem to have suffered too much as a result.

2. What are the alternatives to landfill sites for disposing of rubbish?

3. What kind of crops replace rain forests as a rule?

4. Can you think of some really major 'earth-moving' and building schemes? What is their impact on the environment?

Different perspectives

5. What might a Greenlander think about global warming?

6. Describe and comment on the photograph below.

Charcoal production with logs cut from the Amazon rainforest

Indonesia Plants 79 Million Trees

Kathy Marks

The Indonesian President, Susilo Bambang Yudhoyono, plants a sapling in Jonggol, west Java

Indonesia has embarked on a grand scheme to plant 79 million trees in an attempt to boost its green credentials. [...] President Susilo Bambang Yudhoyono, who was photographed this week planting saplings with government ministers declared that "illegal logging is our biggest enemy" and
5 added: "We will show Indonesia's strong commitment and action to preserve the environment and save our planet."
Environmentalists, however, were unimpressed. In recent years, Indonesia has been destroying its forests at a faster rate than any other country. As a consequence, it has the dubious distinction of being the world's third-big-
10 gest producer of greenhouse gases, behind the US and China. As for its commitment to cracking down on illegal logging, which is a massive problem in Indonesia, one of the nation's most notorious timber barons, Adelin Lis, recently walked free from court. [...]
According to some estimates, Indonesia loses an area of forest the size of
15 Switzerland every year, or the equivalent of a football pitch every ten seconds. Much of it is cleared to make way for lucrative palm oil plantations. Forest fires, land clearing and the degradation of carbon-rich peatlands are blamed for the country's alarming volume of greenhouse gas emissions. Indonesia, which has 10 per cent of the world's remaining tropical rainfor-
20 ests, has called on rich nations to give it financial assistance to preserve them. [Indonesia is also interested in] a carbon trading scheme. [...]
Globally, deforestation is said to contribute one-fifth of all CO_2 emissions – more than the world's cars, trucks, trains and aircraft combined. [...]

Activities

1. Make notes on the article and turn them into a one-paragraph summary.

2. Why do you think Adelin Lis didn't go to prison?

3. List and explain the activities in Indonesia which lead to the "alarming volume of greenhouse gas emissions" (l. 18).

4. Will planting saplings help the situation? Give reasons for your answer.

5. What could be achieved by 'financial assistance'? What would the risks be?

6. How would a carbon trading scheme work?

7. Is what happens in Indonesia any of our business? How are the forests doing in Germany?

8. What features of the article suggest that Kathy Marks is a **good journalist** who has **done her homework**, and **really cares** about the issue? Try to comment on and find examples for each of the items in bold type.

What's it all about?

Can it be stopped?

She really means it

The Dead Heart

Midnight Oil

Midnight Oil was an Australian rock band from Sydney which became famous in the 1980s. 'Midnight Oil' is what you 'burn' when you stay up late working for exams etc. A number of the group's singles and albums were in the Australian top ten, and they won many other awards in their own part of the world and later internationally. Their main themes were politics, consumerism, nuclear issues and the environment. The band broke up in 2002.

In 'The Dead Heart' this white group takes on the persona of indigenous people (here presumably the Australian aborigines) who have been disinherited by white settlers, but still carry in their hearts 'the true country ... that cannot be stolen'.

We don't serve your country
Don't serve your king
Know your custom don't speak your tongue
White man came took everyone

We don't serve your country   5
Don't serve your king
White man listen to the songs we sing
White man came took everything

Chorus:
We carry in our hearts the true country   10
And that cannot be stolen
We follow in the steps of our ancestry
And that cannot be broken

We don't serve your country
Don't serve your king   15
Know your custom don't speak your tongue
White man came took everyone

We don't need protection
Don't need your hand
Keep your promise on where we stand   20
We will listen we'll understand

Chorus (2x)

Mining companies, pastoral[1] companies
Uranium companies
Collected companies   25
Got more right than people
Got more say than people
Forty thousand years can make a difference
   to the state of things
The dead heart lives here   30

_____

[1] **pastoral** literally means using land to graze sheep when used in this kind of context; probably refers here to large-scale farming

Activities

1. 'The speaker clearly sees the environment as a racial issue.' Try to find evidence for this statement in the text.

   A racial issue

2. List the comments made by the speaker about
   a) the white man,
   b) his own people.

3. Explain the third four-line verse (lines 10–13) in your own words.

4. Why should one treat the fairly distant past as if it is the present?

   Problems

5. Discuss the statement 'Forty thousand years can make a difference'.

6. Try to explain the title – and the second reference to the 'dead heart' at the end of the text.

7. List some examples of non-standard English in the song. Who might speak like this? What effect does this kind of language have on the reader/listener?

   What kind of language?

China's Giant Dams

Jim Yardley

You might think that dams are to do with water. Well, that's true, of course, but the great dam projects in China also have a lot to do with land. What, for example?

Before you read

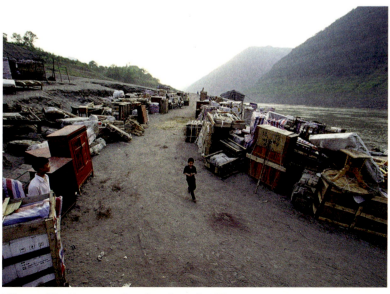

Villagers of Yun Yuang were forced to relocate in 2001

Last year, Chinese officials celebrated the completion of the Three Gorges Dam by releasing a list of 10 world records. As in: The Three Gorges is the world's biggest dam, biggest power plant and biggest consumer of dirt[1], stone, concrete and steel. Ever. Even the project's official tally[2] of 1.13 million displaced people made the list as record No. 10. [...]   5

Few if any hydropower projects have been more controversial than the Three Gorges. Entire cities were inundated[3] along with ancient temples and other landmarks. Today, many of the people resettled by the project are still struggling to survive. For years, despite the problems, Chinese officials rarely criticized the project or expressed concern. And then, unexpectedly, 10 the silence broke. [...]

(Leading officials began to mention 'hidden dangers' which could lead to disaster if left untended[4]; e. g. water pollution, landslides, silting up[5] of the reservoir floor, even a major earthquake induced by rising water behind the dams.)   15

What do you make of ▶ the two figures quoted for displaced persons (here and in the first paragraph)?

In his 2007 work report to the National People's Congress, Prime Minister Wen noted that dam building, over many years, has displaced 23 million people in China. The Three Gorges was supposed to be a model program that would not just move people but also rebuild communities. Resettlement began in 1997 as an upward migration. Farmers could relocate to 20 newly built cities or stay on the farm, albeit[6] on higher ground. But studies now show the region's population density is almost twice the national average. In many villages, too many farmers are perched[7] on steep slopes[8], sharing too little land.

The upward migration also damaged the environment. Farmers cleared 25 land to plant crops or rows of orange trees. Deforestation contributed to soil erosion and destabilized many hillsides. Today, construction crews are busy reinforcing crumbling hillsides above the reservoir with concrete. [...] To further ease pressure on the land, Three Gorges officials changed the relocation policy, promising free land and financial help for people who 30 moved to other provinces.

But leaving the region was not a good solution for many farmers – or a permanent one. More than 100,000 people left, but thousands have since returned, despite no longer holding local residency permits.

"We tried to grow rice in Jiangxi," said Lin Shengping, 51, who left the re- 35 gion but returned to Daqiao where her adult children had stayed. "The harvest was really small. So we all came back. We don't have money, either in Jiangxi or here. But at home I can take care of my grandchildren so my son and daughter-in-law can go out to work."

Around daybreak on June 22, Lu Youbing awoke to the screams of her broth- 40 er-in-law and the sickening sensation of the earth collapsing. Her mountain farmhouse in Jianmin Village buckled as a landslide swept it downhill. In all, 20 homes were demolished. Five months later, Ms. Lu is living in a tent, fending off[9] rats and wondering where her family can go. [...]

What rhetorical device ▶ is used in the last sentence?

[Her tent is] pitched on the only available flat land – a terrace with a monu- 45 ment celebrating efforts by local officials to improve the environment.

---

[1] **dirt** AE for BE earth   [2] **tally** count   [3] **to inundate** to flood   [4] **untended** no action taken   [5] **silt** sand or earth deposited at the bottom of rivers and lakes   [6] **albeit** although, however   [7] **perched** in a high or unsafe position   [8] **slope** hillside   [9] **to fend off** to keep away (with one's hands or a weapon)

Activities

1. Explain the purpose of the Three Gorges Dam scheme in your own words.

A giant project

2. List some of the 'world record' statistics associated with the scheme. How far do you think the Chinese government is right to be proud of these statistics?

3. Find evidence that the project was not very well-planned in some respects.

4. In what ways is the environment affected by this project?

The environment

5. How important are individuals for the Chinese planners?

6. Part of the way through the article there is a sudden change of style and approach on the part of the author. Where does this happen, and what exactly changes?

Style and approach

7. Why do you think the author decided to do this?

8. What would happen if a project like this was planned in Germany (think in terms of new motorways, airports, etc.)?

Your views

9. Why do you think reactions would be so different?

Greenland: Two Views

What do you make of the graph below – and how do you think the information in it was obtained?

Before you read

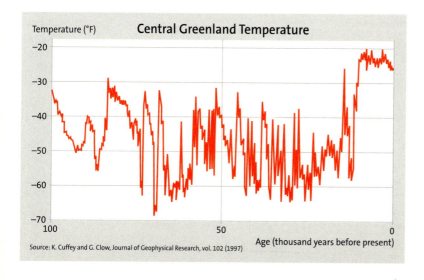

Central Greenland Temperature

Temperature (°F)

Age (thousand years before present)

Source: K. Cuffey and G. Clow, Journal of Geophysical Research, vol. 102 (1997)

Greenland Goes Green – Again

Sara Lyall

Greenland, a self-governing province of Denmark, was settled by the Viking Erik the Red in the 10th century, after his murderous ways got him ejected from Iceland. There were forests and fertile soil then, and the Vikings grew crops and raised sheep for hundreds of years. But temperatures dropped precipitously[1] in the so-called Little Ice Age, which began in the 16th century, the Norse settlers died out and agriculture was no longer possible.

These days [...] the growing season lasts about three weeks longer than a decade ago.

"Now spring is coming earlier, and you can have earlier lambings[2] and longer grazing periods," said Eenoraq Frederiksen, 68, a sheep farmer. [...] A Greenlandic supermarket is stocking locally grown cauliflower, broccoli and cabbage for the first time. Eight sheep farmers are growing potatoes commercially. Five more are experimenting with vegetables. And Kenneth Hoeg, the region's agricultural adviser, says he does not see why southern Greenland cannot eventually be full of vegetable farms and viable[3] forests. [...]

Why mention the ▶ strawberries? Scattered reports of successful strawberry crops in the odd[4] home garden are heard, although it helps to keep them in perspective. As Hans Gronborg, a Danish horticulturalist put it, laughing, "They know whether they've harvested 20 strawberries, or 25."

[1] **precipitously** a long way, very rapidly   [2] **lambing** the time of year (early spring) when lambs are born   [3] **viable** (here) healthy, commercially successful   [4] **odd** (here) a few, here and there

History as Ice-Story

Elizabeth Kolbert

Much of what is known about the earth's climate over the last hundred thousand years comes from the ice cores[1] drilled in central Greenland, along a line known as the ice divide. Owing to differences between summer and winter snow, each layer in a Greenland core can be individually dated, like the rings of a tree. Then, by analyzing the isotopic[2] composition of the ice, it is possible to determine how cold it was at the time each layer was formed. Over the last decade, three Greenland cores have been drilled to a depth of nearly two miles, and these cores have prompted a wholesale rethinking of how the climate operates. Where once the system was thought

Why 'as it were'? ▶ to change, as it were, only glacially, now it is known to be capable of sudden and unpredictable reversals. One such reversal, called the Younger Dryas, after a small Arctic plant [...] that suddenly reappeared in Scandinavia, took place roughly 12,800 years ago. At that point, the earth, which had been

[1] **core** (here) long vertical sample of ice cut out with a hollow drill   [2] **isotopic** (here) based on tiny differences

warming rapidly, was plunged back
15 into ice age conditions. It remained
frigid for twelve centuries and then
warmed again, even more abruptly.
In Greenland, annual average temperatures shot up by nearly twenty
20 degrees in a single decade. [...]
The previous interglacial [period],
which is known as the Eemian,
was somewhat warmer than the
present one, the Holocene. [...] Sea
25 levels during that time were at least
fifteen feet higher than they are today. One theory attributes this to a
collapse of the West Antarctic ice
sheet. A second holds that meltwa-
30 ter from Greenland was responsi-
ble. (When sea ice melts, it does not affect sea level, because the ice, which
was floating, was already displacing an equivalent volume of water.) All
told, the Greenland ice sheet holds enough water to raise sea levels worldwide by twenty-three feet. Scientists at NASA have calculated that through-
35 out the 1990s the ice sheet, despite some thickening at the centre, was
shrinking by twelve cubic miles per year.

◀ Why might this be?

Activities

1. Describe the history of Greenland's climate from the 10th century to the present day in two or three sentences.

    Lyall

2. Explain how Greenland's farmers regard the present-day warming of their country.

3. To what extent are they worried about possible worldwide consequences?

4. Summarise the information which is provided by an analysis of the ice cores.

    Kolbert

5. What do they tell us specifically about the climate in Greenland (and elsewhere on the planet)?

6. What is the most surprising finding, and why should we be concerned about it?

7. Outline and contrast the different views expressed in the two texts. Why do you think there is so little agreement between the two authors?

    Quite a contrast

8. Whose side are you on? Try to give reasons for your choice.

9. What kinds of material are the extracts taken from? Try to find evidence for your answer in the texts.

"An environmental classic." —Time

A Novel

ECOTOPIA
ERNEST CALLENBACH

Ecotopia

Ernest Callenbach

This extract is taken from a Utopian novel which first appeared in 1975, set in the year 1999. The title tells you the kind of utopia Callenbach wrote about. What would you expect from the title? The storyteller is a journalist called Weston, the first 'normal' American to enter Ecotopia, an area in the south-west, which has broken away from the rest of the US, and has introduced border controls etc. to protect it from the unhealthy lifestyle (in the view of the author) of the rest of the country. As in some other Utopian novels written by men, the women in Ecotopia tend to be healthy and attractive, and not averse to an affair with the visitor from another world. Other features of Ecotopia include alternative energy production, slow electric cars, acceptance of soft drug use, systematic recycling and the innovative use of wood-based biodegradable plastics. The education system is very free and flexible, with children spending a lot of time in the open air learning 'survival skills'. The competitive element in school and at work has more or less disappeared.

Here is a brief summary of the contents:

Together with Weston, who at the beginning is curious about, but not particularly sympathetic to, Ecotopia, we learn about the ecotopian train system, life style, war sports, politics (the president is a woman, Vera Allwen), gender relations, sexual freedom, energy production, (organic) agriculture, education, and so on. Ecotopian citizens are characterized as free-thinking, creative and energetic, but also socially responsible and often inclined to work in team configurations. In the end, Weston becomes an Ecotopian himself. (from: www.en.wikipedia.org)

The Assistant Minister is, like many Ecotopians, unnervingly[1] relaxed, with a deep, slow voice. He sprawled[2] on woven cushions in a sunny corner of the floor, under a skylight with some kind of ivy hanging near it, and his lab assistant produced hot water for tea on a bunsen burner. I squatted awk- 5
wardly, and began by asking my carefully prepared questions about Ecotopian agricultural output. These were ignored. Instead the Assistant Minister insisted on giving me "a little background." He then began to discuss, not agriculture at all, but sewage. The first major project of his ministry after Independence, he said, had been to put the country's food cycle on a stable-state basis: all food wastes, sewage[3] and garbage[4] were to be turned 10
into organic fertilizer and applied to the land, where it would again enter into the food production cycle. Every Ecotopian household, thus, is required to compulsively sort all its garbage into compostable[5] and recyclable categories, at what must be an enormous expenditure of personal effort; and expanded fleets of garbage trucks are also needed. 15
The sewage system inherited from the past, according to the Assistant Minister, could only be called a "disposal" system. In it sewage and industrial

Why make tea on a ▶ bunsen burner?

What do the words ▼ 'compulsively', 'enormous expenditure' and 'expanded fleets' tell you about Weston's attitude to Ecotopia at this point?

---

[1] **unnervingly** making other people nervous   [2] **sprawled** half sitting, half lying   [3] **sewage** what goes down the toilet and into the drains   [4] **garbage** mainly US word for rubbish
[5] **compostable** able to be turned into compost, i. e. to become a rich, organic product very popular with gardeners, cf. the compost heap, to be found in most gardens

wastes had not been productively recycled but merely dumped, in a more
or less toxic condition, into rivers, bays and oceans. This, he maintained,
20 was not only dangerous to the public health and the life of water creatures,
but its very objective was wasteful and unnatural. With a smile, he added
that some of the sewage practices of earlier days would even be considered
criminal if carried out today. [...]

"After seven years we were able to dispense with chemical fertilizers en-
25 tirely. This was partly through sewage recycling, partly through garbage
composting, and partly through [other means]. You may have seen from the
train that our farm animals are not kept in close confinement like yours.
We like them to live in conditions approaching the natural. But not only for
sentimental reasons. It also avoids the gigantic accumulation of manure
30 which is such a problem in your feedlots[6] and poultry factories."

Naturally, this smug[7] account roused all my skepticism, and I questioned
him about the economic drawbacks of such a system. My questions, however, met a flat denial. "On the contrary," he replied, "our system is consid-
erably cheaper than yours, if we add in *all* the costs. Many of your costs are
35 ignored, or passed on through subterfuge[8] to posterity or the general public. We on the other hand must acknowledge all costs. Otherwise we could
not hope to achieve the stable-state life systems which are our fundamental
ecological and political goal. If, for instance, we had continued your prac-
tice of 'free' disposal of wastes in watercourses, sooner or later somebody
40 else would have had to calculate (and bear) the costs of the resulting dead
rivers and lakes. We prefer to do it ourselves. It is obviously not easy to
quantify certain of these costs. But we have been able to approximate them
in workable political terms – especially since our country is relatively sensible in scale." [...]

45 Next I asked the Assistant Minister about Ecotopian food production and
processing. I knew he must be aware of the great achievements of our food
industry in recent decades, not only in the introduction of synthetic meat
and other protein foods, but also in pre-cooking and packaging generally. I
was curious to see how he would justify the regressive practices that, acc-
50 ording to many rumors, had returned Ecotopian agriculture to the dark
ages, and cooks to their chopping blocks and hot stoves (microwave ovens
being illegal in Ecotopia).

◀ What are the
implications of 'relatively
sensible in scale'?

---

[6] **feedlot** a relatively small piece of land or building where animals are fattened up as
quickly as possible [7] **smug** a smug person is very pleased with him/herself – and it
shows [8] **subterfuge** a dishonest plan intended to conceal the truth

Activities

1. Explain how a 'stable-state' basis for Ecotopian agriculture was
   achieved.

2. Compare this system with the system in Germany.

3. Summarise the minister's views of the American 'disposal system'.

4. Explain the difference between the terms 'disposal' and 'recycling'.

Waste 'disposal' good
and bad

5. Why is the American 'disposal' system not as cheap as it seems?

Back to the dark
ages?
6. We know that Weston decides to stay in Ecotopia at the end of his visit. In what areas do you think he will have to change his ideas?

7. The young men of Ecotopia take part in war games at regular intervals – and some of them actually get injured with spears. Why might Callenbach have felt it necessary to introduce this kind of activity?

Are you the Eco-
topian type?
8. On the basis of the information in the introduction and in the text, how would you feel about living in an Ecotopia-type world? Write a paragraph in which you discuss the pros and cons and try to come to a conclusion.

Saving London

Juliette Jowit

Before you read
What do you know about the Thames barrier? What is its purpose and how does it work?

The Thames Barrier

The cost of protecting London and the south-east from flooding will be at least £4bn as sea levels rise and the south-east coast sinks over the next century, a report for the Environment
5 Agency has warned.
Experts have recognized that the Thames Barrier should be able to guard against the possibility of a major flood until 2030, but say that billions need to be spent on raising 300 km of other de-
10 fences to protect the capital – and even more than that if the sea level rises still further.
At worst, the cost of a major new barrier would be 'in excess of £20bn', says the report by the Thames Estuary 2100 project team.

The report – which goes further than previous 15 warnings – is the latest example of huge bills which face British taxpayers and people around the world to protect themselves from the expected impacts of climate change.
The more we curb emissions [blamed for global 20 warming], therefore, the less investment will be required in extreme measures[1] to combat the increasing risk from sea-level rise and climate change, adds the report.
Dave Wardle, the EA's area manager for the 25 Thames region, said the report showed that the Thames Barrier, opened in 1982, had been well designed and maintained, but that the agency would need more money from government in future. Damage is currently £1bn a year, said the 30 EA.
The report also said the Environment Agency's Making Space for Water strategy, which aims to find land which can store floodwater, from parks to car parks, could extend the life of the Thames 35 Barrier by 50 to 80 years beyond 2030.
The report's findings are based on the government estimate that the average rise in sea level by 2100 will be 0.94 metres, although it also considered higher estimates of up to 4.2 metres. 40 About 1 mm a year of the increase is due to geological changes, as southern England subsides;

---
[1] **measures** steps which will need to be taken

the rest is because global warming is causing ice to melt and seawater to expand, said Professor
45 Jim Hall of Newcastle University, who has advised the EA on flood risk in the region.

'These are pretty conservative scenarios, but London is an important place, so it's important they look at some far-out what-ifs[2] – even if these are not the basis for the design.'
50

---

[2] **far-out what-ifs** things which seem very unlikely or in the realm of science fiction (at present) but could happen and would need strategies to deal with them

Activities

1. List global reasons why the Thames Barrier will sooner or later become out of date.

   Holding back the floods

2. Explain the 'Making Space for Water' strategy. How could it help to extend the life of the Thames Barrier?

3. What specific reasons are given for rising water levels in southern England (don't mention global warming in general)?

4. Name some other areas which are likely to suffer from rising sea levels.

   It's not just London

5. How would you characterise some of these areas?

6. As you know, global efforts to combat global warming seem unlikely to have very much effect. How should we try to deal with them – or can you think of ways in which we might after all avoid at least some of the consequences? Write a paragraph in which you express your personal views on the issues.

   Should we accept the inevitable?

7. How can the cartoon below be related to the text about the Thames Barrier? Be careful – it's a catch question!

Arctic Sea Ice Is Melting – Fast!

Steve Connor

A very pretty picture, but ...

[This year – 2007] the sea ice of the Arctic will melt further and faster than at any time since records began nearly 30 years ago according to the latest data collected by a satellite survey of the polar region. [...]

This year has seen one of the most rapid rates of sea ice melting, which began in spring after one of the most disappointing winters for ice forma- 5 tion. "Unless something unusual happens we're definitely on track for[1] a record loss of sea ice. We're on track to shatter[2] all records," said Mark Serreze, an Arctic specialist at the US National Snow and Ice Data Centre at Colorado University in Denver. "The rates of sea ice loss this year are really rather remarkable. Some of the daily rates of loss are the biggest we've ever 10 seen. Things are happening really fast," Dr Serreze said. [...]

In July of this year, more sea ice melted than for any month on record. The surface area covered by the ice in July was 3.13 million square miles, about 347,492 square miles below the area recorded for July 2005 – an area seven times the size of England. 15

[...] Some computer models used by the UN's Intergovernmental Panel on Climate Change predict the Arctic will be virtually[3] ice free by the summer of 2070. However, other computer models suggest that the year of an ice-free arctic summer could come as early as 2030 or 2040.

Dr Serreze said that even these pessimistic predictions may have over- 20 estimated the resilience[4] of the Arctic sea ice. He said that we may have already reached the tipping point[5] when there is a rapid disintegration. [...]

Most polar specialists agree that as more ice is lost in summer, the Arctic is liable to heat up faster than normal as a result of a positive feedback in the

---

[1] **on track for** on course for, well on the way to   [2] **to shatter** to break (in a dramatic way/into small pieces)   [3] **virtually** almost   [4] **resilience** (here) ability to recover   [5] **tipping point** point at which there is a sudden change in a process, possibly also a point of no return

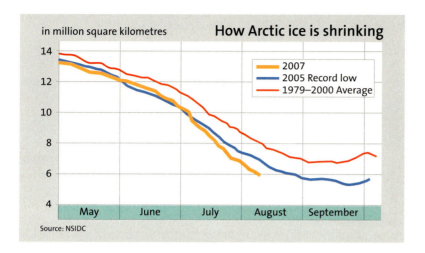

in million square kilometres — **How Arctic ice is shrinking**

Legend:
- 2007
- 2005 Record low
- 1979–2000 Average

Source: NSIDC

25 climate – instead of solar energy being reflected from the surface of the white ice, it is absorbed by the open, darker ocean, leading to even more melting of the ice. [...] Polar bears, which rely on sea ice to hunt for seals in summer, are already showing signs of malnutrition, because they have to swim further between the ice floes[6]. Scientists believe the species could
30 quickly go extinct if there is no sea ice at all in summer. Paradoxically, the loss of sea ice will give Arctic countries such as Russia, Denmark, Canada, Norway and the US easier access to the parts of the seabed that are thought to be rich in oil and gas – the same fossil fuels that have exacerbated[7] the global warming that has caused the sea ice to melt in the first place.

◄ **Why is Denmark on this list?**

---

[6] **ice floe** *Eisscholle*   [7] **to exacerbate** to make worse

Activities

1. What is the general reason for the Arctic ice melting?

2. Outline and comment on the information on the graph.

3. Explain how the winter of 2007–2008 could be 'disappointing' (line 5).

4. Why does the exposure of more surface seawater lead to even faster melting of the ice?

5. Comment on the fact that there is no mention of rising sea levels.

6. Explain in your own words the paradox referred to near the end of the article.

7. What other groups might be pleased to discover less and less ice in the Arctic?

8. Comment on the style of the article. Does it match up well with the subject matter? Where would you expect an article of this kind to appear?

Let's get this straight

The paradox

Dramatic stuff

Floating Houses

Elizabeth Kolbert

Floating homes in the Netherlands

The town of Maasbommel [...] lies on the banks of the River Meuse and is a popular holiday destination; every summer it fills with tourists who have come to go boating or to camp out. Thanks to the risk of flooding, building is restricted 5 along the river, but a few years ago one of the Netherlands' largest construction firms received permission to turn a former RV[1] park on the banks of the Meuse into a development of "amphibious homes". [...] 10

The amphibious homes all look alike. They are tall and narrow, with flat sides and curved metal roofs, so that standing next to one another they resemble a row of toasters. Each one is moored[2] to a metal pole and sits on a set of hollow con- 15 crete pontoons[3].

Assuming that all goes to plan, when the Meuse floods, the homes will bob up[4] and then, when the water recedes, they will gently be deposited back on land. At the point that I visited, half a 20 dozen families were occupying their amphibious houses. Anna van der Molen, a nurse and mother of four, gave me a tour of hers. She was enthusiastic about life on the river. "Not one day is the same," she told me. In the future, she said, she expected that people all over the world would live in floating houses, since, as she put it, "the water is coming up, and we have 25 to live with it, not fight it – it's just not possible."

---

[1] **RV** recreational vehicle (*Wohnmobil*)   [2] **moored** tied/attached to a solid object with ropes etc. like a boat   [3] **pontoon** a floating section of a harbour, bridge etc. which can go up and down with changing water levels   [4] **to bob up** (here) to start to float

Activities

It's not science fiction!

1. Describe one of these floating houses for someone who has not seen the photos above.

2. What problem are they designed to solve?

Other solutions

3. What other solutions can you think of to the problems of living on the water or in areas subject to flooding?

My home is my (floating) castle

4. Write a brief essay about the pros and cons of living in a floating house (novelty value? garden? getting ashore when the water rises? stormy weather?).

5. Discuss your views with other students.

The War against the Trees

Stanley Kunitz

The man who sold his lawn to Standard Oil
Joked with his neighbours come to watch the show
While the bulldozers, drunk with gasoline,
Tested the virtue[1] of the soil
5 Under the branchy sky
By overthrowing first the privet-row.

Forsythia[2]-forays[3] and hydrangea-raids
Were but preliminaries to a war
Against the great-grandfathers of the town,
10 So freshly lopped[4] and maimed[5].
They struck and struck again,
And with each elm a century went down.

All day the hireling[6] engines charged the trees,
Subverting[7] them by hacking underground
15 In grub-dominions[8], where dark summer's mole
Rampages[9] through his halls,
Till a northern seizure[10] shook
Those crowns, forcing the giants to their knees.

I saw the ghosts of children at their games
20 Racing beyond their childhood in the shade,
And while the green world turned its death-foxed[11] page
And a red wagon wheeled,
I watched them disappear
Into the suburbs of their grievous age[12].

25 Ripped from the craters much too big for hearts
The club-roots[13] bared[14] their amputated coils[15],
Raw gorgons[16] matted[17] blind, whose pocks[18] and scars[19]
Cried moon! on a corner lot
One witness-moment, caught
30 In the rear-view mirrors of the passing cars.

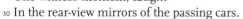

---

[1] **tested the virtue** the poet sees cutting down the trees as rape (*Vergewaltigung*)
[2] **forsythia/hydrangea** common shrubs (*Ziersträucher*)   [3] **foray** a short, sudden attack
[4] **to lop** to cut off branches   [5] **maimed** badly injured, (usually refers to the loss of one or more limbs)   [6] **hireling** sb. working for someone else, often on a temporary basis (usually refers to an unreliable worker)   [7] **to subvert** to undermine   [8] **grub-dominions** underground areas inhabited by grubs (*Larven*)   [9] **to rampage** to rush around angrily
[10] **a northern seizure** the crowns of the trees start to shake as they begin to fall   [11] **death-foxed** covered with brownish spots like very old paper   [12] **grievous age** old age is seen as a time of suffering   [13] **club-roots** roots in the shape of clubs (*Keulen*)   [14] **to bare** (here) to shake free of earth   [15] **coil** snakes and springs (*Federn*) often form coils   [16] **gorgon** a mythical, very ugly female monster with snakes instead of hair; anyone looking at her would be turned into stone   [17] **matted** twisted together, tangled (*verfilzt*), often mixed with other material (mud, blood)   [18] **pocks** (here) small craters   [19] **scars** the marks left when wounds have healed

Activities

What's it all about?

1. Explain what the poem is about in three or four sentences.

2. Have a look at the first two lines. How does the tone differ from the rest of the poem?

3. Now have a look at the last two lines. What new perspective do they add to the scene?

Poetry versus prose

4. The poem is full of emotionally-charged words. Make a list of the most striking ones.

5. How do these words tell you what the poet feels about the trees being cut down?

6. Which parts of the poem convey the idea that a 'war' is being waged against the trees?

7. The fourth verse could be described as visionary. Why do you think the poet refers to the 'ghosts' of children?

We're (nearly) all environmentalists now

8. Choose an environmental issue or event which makes or has made you really angry. Try to write a really impassioned short article about it, using some emotive language to reinforce your case, as Kunitz has done.

Air and energy

Producing Energy

The drawings in the 'picture gallery' below show some of the main ways in which we produce energy. Name them, and say something about their effect on the environment (if any)?

Before you read

Conventional or Alternative?

Supporters of conventional or alternative forms of power could each use the photograph below to support their cases. Which side are you on, and how would you support your case, using the photograph as a starting point for an informal debate?

Cars, Cars, Cars

Stephen Speight

We all know that cars (and other motor vehicles, of course) are bad for the environment: carbon dioxide, carbon monoxide, diesel fumes ... and then there's the little problem that the fuel they drink so thirstily is beginning to run out.

Because, collectively, we have a bad conscience, we are belatedly taking 5 steps to make cars cleaner and more economical. Not very big steps, though.

For every economy model at the bottom of a manufacturer's range, there tends to be another mighty behemoth[1] at the top of the range. Those of you 10 who are interested in cars might like to look at the ranges of some major car manufacturers, and report back to your class on the most – and least – economical models on offer. The others could 15 discuss the implications of the photo, taken, where else, in China.

---

[1] **behemoth** a huge mythical beast/monster; may in the past also have referred to a hippopotamus (*Nilpferd*)

There's a good side to the picture, too. The car has brought mobility, pleasure and pride in ownership to hundreds of millions of people worldwide, and we're not going to give up our cars without a tremendous struggle. (Nearly) everyone hopes we won't have to. Here's a photograph taken at one of the big motor shows, complete with shiny bonnet[2], girls, photographers, journalists – all the usual razzmatazz[3], in fact. How do you react to it?

The photo below adds another factor to the mix. Greenpeace activists believe that German high performance cars (and the people who make them) are responsible for more than their fair share of carbon dioxide emissions. It is true that French and Italian manufacturers produce a lot more small, economical cars than the German car industry, and the Japanese were first with a hybrid car which wasn't just a prototype. But Germany's car industry is proud of its reputation for high quality and high performance. It's Germany's USP (unique selling proposition). Without this reputation, and cars to match, the German economy would be in deep trouble. Why else have successive governments refused to impose a speed limit on the *Autobahn*? Some commentators feel that Germany should have taken more of a lead in producing clean, economical cars.

The French were well ahead in producing particle filters for diesel engines, for example, and Germany was left 'playing catch-up' for a couple of years. The word 'premium' is generally used to describe cars towards the top end of the market. Is it possible for Germany to keep its leading position in the worldwide premium segment of the market, and at the same time take the lead in making clean, economical cars? Most German cars produce more CO_2 than the levels which the EU intends to impose.

And what role do SUVs play in the equation? The cartoon has something to say about that.

A pink protest from Greenpeace

---

[2] **bonnet** (here) *Motorhaube* (originally an old-fashioned ladies' hat)   [3] **razzmatazz** a lot of noisy, showy activity

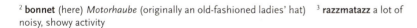

Activities

1. Collect some statements from your class about the quality and image of German cars.

2. Do the same for foreign cars (sort the statements according to the other main car-manufacturing countries).

3. Discuss the future of the German car industry on this basis, taking into account the increasing impact of high fuel prices and environmental issues.

4. Germany is proud of its record on recycling and other environmental issues, but there's no general speed limit on the *Autobahn*. Write a short speech for or against such a speed limit, and use it in an informal class debate on the issue.

Let's get technical

5. What is the problem with CO_2? After all, it's just the stuff which makes fizzy drinks fizzy, isn't it?

6. How does a hybrid car work?

7. Could electric cars be the answer?

8. To what extent are diesel engines better for the environment than petrol engines?

9. What role does driving style play in saving fuel?

You and your car

10. What kind of car would you like to own one day? Or would you rather own no car at all? Or a motor-cycle? If you like, you can choose a dream car and a more practical car. Explain your choice(s) to your fellow-students.

Personal transport – the future

11. What do you think cars will be like half a century from now? Or won't there be any?

12. What is the message of the cartoon on the previous page?

13. The photo below shows the world's cheapest car, the Tata Nano, which its Indian makers hope will mobilise their vast nation. Find out more about this car, and try to assess its potential, good or bad.

A Car-lover's Lament

Chris Chilton

For many people living in industrial countries, the car has been and still is extremely important. Passing the driving test, buying the first car (usually an 'old banger' unless daddy is rich), using the car as a love-nest, moving on to a new or newish family car, or a sports car for the single, or an SUV, these are rites of passage in our kind of world. For successful people, moving up to the kind of car which functions as a powerful status symbol is also an important step. And at every stage there is an element of fun, excitement, pride in ownership, yes, even for the first old banger. So what if in future we have to see the car entirely in practical, economical, environmental terms? That's the issue which Chris Chilton, who writes for one of the most prestigious British car magazines, deals with below.

Forget coupé-cabrios, crossovers[1] and luxury off-roaders. If you're a large car manufacturer, the latest must-have accessory in your showroom is the economy car [...] – a lightly-modified production car, usually diesel-powered and tweaked[2] to eke out[3] a couple more mpg[4] and emit a few less noxious
5 g/km.
We tried Volkswagen's Polo Bluemotion in the July 2007 issue, but in the past few months, Audi, Volvo and Seat have all announced such cars, the key ingredients of which seem to be taller gearing[5] and low rolling resistance tyres.
10 Now I can imagine that the hardcore[6] enthusiasts among you are worried at this news. You're thinking that if this catches on, by 2015 we'll all be driving cars fitted with remanufactured Citroën 2CV rubber[7] and cogs[8] so tall we'll have to park on hills to stand any chance of pulling away again. [...]

---

[1] **crossover** car which combines the characteristics of two conventional vehicles, e. g. coupé and off-roader   [2] **to tweak** improve performance by means of minor changes   [3] **to eke out** to make something last as long as possible   [4] **mpg** miles per gallon (of fuel)   [5] **taller gearing** higher gearing, i. e. less engine revolutions per km, resulting in better economy   [6] **hardcore** (here) not likely to change one's views   [7] **2CV rubber** very thin tyres as fitted to the 2CV ("*Ente*")   [8] **cogs** gears

Cars today are faster, safer, quieter, greener and better-built than ever before. But I can't help wondering if the need to be greener, safer and more socially responsible might see us reach some sort of tipping point in the near future. A point which we will later recognise as the time when cars became less good.

Of course, cars will continue to become safer, quieter and greener and all those other politically correct things. But what about the fun element? [...] It's a difficult one to get your head around. On the one hand, as a sane human being I want to minimise damage to the planet and reduce road fatalities[9]. But as a car enthusiast I'm worried that the pleasure derived from future cars will all be related to the quality of the leather covering the car-to-car communication interface rather than that derived from actually driving.

Maybe I'll become some sort of Mad Max renegade[10], leading a bunch of car-mad loonies on a rampage[11], tearing from one end of the country to the other (in a very fast, noisy, thirsty old car). Or maybe I'll just kowtow[12], slip into my 2040 BMW H5, press GO and catch up with the (digital) papers as it joins the motorway car train to London. [...]

---

[9] **road fatalities** people killed on the roads   [10] **renegade** someone who ignores the laws of the land in a dramatic kind of way   [11] **to be on a/the rampage** to rush around damaging things   [12] **to kowtow** to accept with resignation/humility (originally a Chinese custom – bowing until one's forehead touches the ground)

Activities

What's his problem?

1. Explain in two or three sentences what worries the author about the trend towards more environmentally-acceptable cars.

2. What does he mean by a 'tipping point' (line 16)?

3. What two options does he see for himself in the future?

Getting technical

4. Explain how thin tyres and high gearing can save petrol/diesel.

5. If you don't already know about these things, find out what common devices for cleaning up exhaust gases are already fitted to nearly all modern cars, and explain how they work.

6. What might a 'motorway car train' be?

Motoring journalism

7. What features of this article show that it was written by a good motoring journalist for an up-market car magazine?

Car freak or eco-freak?

8. Cars have given people in developed countries a degree of freedom and convenience which they could never have dreamed of a couple of hundred years ago. Now cars are under threat for all kinds of reasons. What is your attitude to cars and driving? Fun, convenience, or something we should learn to do without altogether? Write a paragraph expressing your views, and discuss them with your fellow-students.

The Price of Oil

Rasanter Anstieg

Was waren das noch für Zeiten: Anfang der Siebzigerjahre kostete Öl nur zwei bis drei Dollar pro Fass. Die erste Ölkrise 1973 ließ die Notierung dann in den zweistelligen Bereich schnellen. Seitdem war der Rohstoff nicht mehr für unter 10 Dollar je Fass zu haben. Von Dezember 1998 – damals drückte die Asienkrise den Ölpreis – bis heute hat sich der Kurs fast verzehnfacht.

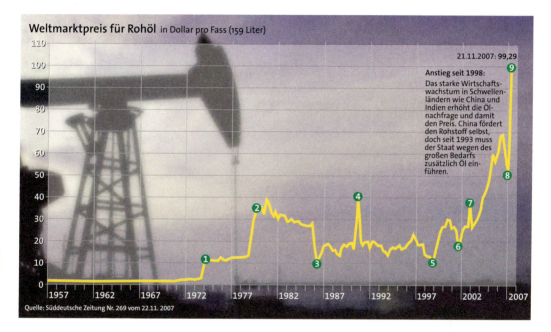

Weltmarktpreis für Rohöl in Dollar pro Fass (159 Liter)

21.11.2007: 99,29

Anstieg seit 1998: Das starke Wirtschaftswachstum in Schwellenländern wie China und Indien erhöht die Ölnachfrage und damit den Preis. China fördert den Rohstoff selbst, doch seit 1993 muss der Staat wegen des großen Bedarfs zusätzlich Öl einführen.

Quelle: Süddeutsche Zeitung Nr. 269 vom 22.11. 2007

① **Januar 1974: 11,57**
Im Herbst 1973 verringert die Organisation erdölexportierender Länder (Opec) die Fördermenge, um den Preis hochzutreiben und damit den Westen unter Druck zu setzen: Die erste Ölkrise beginnt, in Deutschland herrscht an Sonntagen Fahrverbot. Hintergrund ist der sogenannte Jom-Kippur-Krieg zwischen Israel und seinen arabischen Nachbarn.

② **Juni 1979: 35,09**
In dem Jahr stürzt Ajatollah Chomeini in Iran den Schah. Ein Jahr später beginnt der Krieg zwischen Iran und Irak: die zweite Ölkrise.

③ **März 1986: 10,04**
Die weltweite Förderung übersteigt den Bedarf. Opec-Mitglieder scheren aus dem Kartell aus und senken die Preise.

④ **Oktober 1990: 40,85**
Der Zweite Golfkrieg: Im August marschiert der Irak in Kuwait ein. Anfang 1991 erobert eine Koalition unter Führung der USA Kuwait zurück.

⑤ **Dezember 1998: 10,70**
1997 und 1998 belastet die Asienkrise die Weltwirtschaft.

⑥ **November 2001: 17.72**
Die Terroranschläge vom 11. September in den USA bremsen die Weltkonjunktur.

⑦ **Februar 2003: 37,68**
Ein Angriff der USA auf den Irak rückt näher. Im März beginnt der Einmarsch.

⑧ **Januar 2007: 50,50**
Der milde Winter in vielen Industriestaaten dämpft die Nachfrage nach Energie.

Activity

Imagine that a friend who does not speak German sees the interesting graph on p. 33, and asks you to explain the main features of it. You can use the same numbering system.

European Energy Security

'PROVIDING ENERGY SECURITY'

Activity

... And here's another comment on oil (gas = gasoline = BE petrol). The cartoon is from an American newspaper, reprinted from a newspaper published in Dubai. Describe and interpret the cartoon. Can you think of any reasons why a newspaper from that part of the world (U.A.E. = the United Arab Emirates) might publish this cartoon?

Oil Apocalypse

Robin McKie

The text begins with a description of a 'disaster movie' which suggests that we will soon have world-wide 'oil riots' as the world's oil wells begin to dry up with demand and prices continuing to rise. Although the author accepts that easily-available oil stocks may run out in the foreseeable future, he quotes comments from an expert who feels that rising oil prices will make it feasible to exploit many other sources and resources in future.

Oil is 'the bloodstain of the earth's economy' and will soon trigger a global conflict that will cost millions of lives. That is the stark[1] claim of a controversial new film, which says a crash in oil production is about to set off a worldwide recession and economic collapse. *A Crude Awakening: The Oil*
5 *Crash*, which opens in UK cinemas this week, shows stark images of rusting Texan and Venezuelan wells and fuel riots in Asia and Africa. Such scenes will be repeated thousands of times around the planet in the near future, argue the film's makers, who say the world is facing changes 'more frightening than a horror movie'. [...]
10 [The film] is a dramatic depiction of the arguments of economists and geologists who say that the day of 'peak oil' has either occurred or is imminent[2]. Peak oil is defined as the time when the world produces its maximum output of oil and enters a period when prices start to soar[3] as demand rises – thanks in part to the industrialisation of China and India – while supplies dwindle. [...]
15 In the North Sea, oil production has been declining for years, America reached its maximum output decades ago, and in other parts of the world stocks of easily accessible oil are slowly being used up. [...]
Oil companies say that there are still major reserves to be exploited. In particular, Arctic and Antarctic fields – which are being freed of ice and snow
20 as the world heats up – are being sized up for their reserve potential. [...]
It is an alarming scenario, although a note of caution was sounded by John Loughhead, director of the UK Energy Research centre. 'It is true that we may very soon run out of oil from accessible sources, but there are many other types of fuel that we could exploit,' he said.
25 At present, energy companies exploit a field only if they think they can get oil out of the ground at a cost of less than $18 a barrel. This is a very conservative estimate, given current prices. At present oil is being sold at over $90 a barrel. 'If, in future, companies use a more realistic figure of $40 a barrel instead of $18, that would make many, many more reserves sud-
30 denly become economical – the oil tar fields of Alaska, deep water reservoirs, and others,' Loughhead said. [...]
'It is becoming easier and easier to turn substances like coal and gas into liquid form and use that as a substitute for oil, so fuels based on hydrocarbons[4] will still be with us in some form for a few decades yet.

---

[1] **stark** powerful and unpleasant   [2] **imminent** coming soon and usually unpleasant (this is the term used in shipping forecasts for bad weather on the way)   [3] **to soar** to rise rapidly in the air like a bird   [4] **hydrocarbons** high-energy liquid and gaseous compounds of hydrogen and carbon such as petrol, diesel, butane, propane and methane

George, it took me 7 days of hard work to create this planet. Please don't ruin it!

Really, George, I'm disappointed in you.
What you're allowing to happen to my planet is a disgrace.
You claim to have a 'direct line' to me, you've even said,
'I trust that God speaks through me'.
Yet it seems to me it's the oil companies who are speaking through you.
Well George, here's an opportunity to make it up to me.'
When you meet with your fellow World leaders I would like you
to reduce your emissions to save my planet
from being destroyed by climate change.
Can I trust you to do just this one thing for me, George?
For God's sake

Yours everlasting

God

www.forgodssake.org

Activities

Three views

1. Consider the 'letter from God' and the text on page 35 separately. Each of them represents a different viewpoint. Try to express these viewpoints in one or two sentences for each.

Really, George

2. What exactly annoyed the authors of this letter so much about the energy policies of George W. Bush?

3. What do they want him to do to put things right?

4. Would he have been able to do what was necessary (if he had wanted to)?

Oil is the bloodstain

5. The film referred to on p. 35 is a 'disaster movie'. What features would you expect to find in a film of this type?

6. Explain the term 'peak oil'. Why is this an important concept for our world?

7. What is the film's message?

8. Why is Loughhead less worried about dwindling oil supplies from conventional sources than the makers of *A Crude Awakening*?

A note of caution

9. Environmentalists would be worried by some of Loughhead's statements. Which statements, and why?

10. Do you think we will 'run out of oil' (or have to pay really astronomical prices for it) in the fairly near future? Make some notes on your views and discuss them in class.

Why We Must Give up Flying

Nicholas Crane

Nicholas Crane is a well-known TV personality and travel writer, with a special interest in the environment. Ten years ago he decided never to fly again. An extreme view, of course, in an age of cheap flights for ordinary people. What do you think? Before you read the text, try to explain and interpret the cartoon below.

Before you read

In 1988, Crane attended a lecture on the hole in the ozone layer which changed his life.

After the lecture I walked across Hyde Park in the dark, numb[1] with shock. I knew that the atmosphere was thin, but Mother Earth's filtration and re-

---

[1] **numb** without any feeling(s)

cycling systems had always seemed capable of neutralising or absorbing 5
pollutants. The implications of an unstable, perforated[2] atmosphere were
frightening. Then came "global warming". Nothing, but nothing since the
last Ice Age has posed a bigger threat to mankind. Some scientists think
that we may have 10 years to make a sharp reduction in carbon-dioxide
emissions. Others think it is already too late, and that mankind will be 10
lucky to last until the end of the century.

My own culpability in this manmade mess is considerable. For the best part
of 20 years I worked as a travel writer, and although nearly all the books I
wrote were based on journeys by bicycle or on foot, I often flew to my chosen country. From the earliest days of the global warming issue, flying has 15
been implicated as a significant contributor to atmospheric overload. I took
flights to South America, to Africa, to the Caribbean. I once flew to Aus-
tralia for just a week. The articles I wrote tended to fizz[3] with enthusiasm
for the places I had been investigating. I don't know how many readers
booked flights after reading these articles. As I type these words it's impos- 20
sible not to be wracked with[4] guilt.

In 1995, I realised that I would have to stop flying. [...]

In 1996, I tentatively[5] began seeking commissions that I could undertake
by train. I cycled two new bike routes, hiked[6] along the coast of Devon and
took Eurostar to France. [...]   25

In the spring of 1997, I took my last flight as a travel writer. It was to visit
one of the few remaining wolf habitats in Europe, up in the mountain wilderness of Portugal's Trás os Montes. [...]

My conversion to "green journalism" was less alarming than I had antici-
pated. My career didn't grind to a halt[7]. I reacquainted myself with Britain 30
and found a land of many wonders. Newspapers and magazines wanted to
buy stories on [...] fossil-hunting in Dorset and on camping in the Hebrides. I still miss the wider world. There are places that I will never see. Patagonia, Antarctica, [and] Alaska [...] will remain off limits[8] – unless I sail,
cycle and walk there. [...]   35

It's all very well for me to give up air tourism after winging[9] around the
world for a couple of decades. Why shouldn't the next generation have the
same fun? Well, I have no answer to that. [...]

Among the people I know well, the "non-adapters" to climate change are
well-informed adults. I am absolutely mystified[10] by this. It is no longer pos- 40
sible to claim that there is no connection between human activity and climate
change. Or that climate change should be welcomed because it will bring
vineyards to Clydeside. Or that aircraft emissions are good for the planet because they add a reflective heat-shield of pollutants to the atmosphere. [...]

(But) there are other options. Britain and Europe offer a lifetime's worth of 45
travel, all of which can be done by land and sea. Why go to New Zealand if
you haven't seen the sun set over the Hebrides? [...]

---

[2] **perforated** (here) full of holes   [3] **to fizz** (here) to be full of   [4] **to be wracked with (guilt)**
to have powerful (bad) feelings about sth.   [5] **tentatively** trying something and feeling
uncertain about the result   [6] **to hike** *wandern*   [7] **to grind to a halt** to come slowly to a
standstill (like a train)   [8] **off limits** somewhere you are not allowed to go (a military
term)   [9] **to wing** to fly   [10] **mystified** puzzled

Activities

1. Summarise Crane's pre-1998 view of the environment.

2. What caused him to change his mind?

3. Explain why he feels personally responsible for global warming to some extent.

4. How has his life as a travel writer changed since he gave up flying?

5. Explain what Crane means by 'non-adapters' to climate change.

6. List the points which 'non-adapters' make in order to defend their views.

7. Why doesn't he agree with them?

8. "Why shouldn't the next generation have the same fun?" Crane can't answer this question. As members of the 'next generation' what would your answers be?

9. Re-formulate Crane's final question for someone living in Germany, and put it to your fellow-students.

One man's views

A voice crying in the wilderness?

Hard choices

The Last Century for Man

Marillion

Marillion are a British rock group which was formed in 1979. There have been various changes in style and group memberships over the years, but they are still going strong. They were one of the first groups to interact with their fans via the Internet.

This song can be seen as an ironic comment on the 'last century' for our world, but it does not offer any advice on changing course before it is too late.

Here we are
At the beginning of the last century for man
Usin' up parts of the world we haven't even seen or been to
The wretched[1] of the earth exploited by the rich few
5 What's new?

If you are not outraged[2]
You haven't been paying attention
If you are not outraged
You haven't been listening

---

[1] **wretched** poor and unhappy   [2] **outraged** shocked and very angry

10 *Chorus:*
God bless America, I mean it
God bless the UK, I mean it
God bless la belle France, I mean it
And God help us all

15 Climb into the car
I know that makes you happy
The sound of your laughter
Will get you so far
Grace or disgrace
20 Can make you a star these days
Reality pays
Let's decide who the terrorists are

Chorus:
God bless America, I mean it
25 God bless the UK, I mean it
Hats off to China, and India
And Africa too.

Eat all we can
Drink all we can
30 Use all we can
Do what we can
Screw[3] what we can
Don't miss a chance
In the last century for man

35 I wanna feel ALIVE
Gas up[4] the 4 wheel drive! ...

Chorus:
God bless America, I mean it
God bless the UK
40 God bless our children
And God help us all

————————
[3] **to screw** to have sex with, or to wreck/damage/make a mess of sth. (probably both meanings implied)
[4] **to gas up** (AE) to fill up with petrol/gasoline.

Activities

The prose meaning

1. Ignoring the choruses for the moment, explain what the song is about in a few sentences.

2. Tricky expressions.
   Try to explain what is meant by the following expressions:
   • 'If you are not outraged/You haven't been paying attention' (l. 6/7)
   • 'Climb into the car/I know that makes you happy' (l. 15/16)
   • 'Grace or disgrace/Can make you a star these days/Reality pays' (ll. 19–21)
   • 'Let's decide who the terrorists are' (l. 22)

The message

3. The writer seems to be pretty sure that homo sapiens has entered his last century. What makes him so confident?

4. How far do you agree with him?

5. Comment on 'God bless America' and references to other countries mentioned in the choruses.

6. Discuss the singer's views on saving the planet.

A paradox

7. Although the writer clearly knows what we are doing wrong, he seems to be encouraging us to carry on in the same way. How far does this weaken the effect of the song? Write a paragraph on this topic, ending it with your own assessment of the song.

Saving the Planet?

The Global Context

We would (nearly) all like to think that we are doing our bit to save the planet. When we read about something encouraging like the MS *Beluga* (see below) we are pleased because this experiment has all the 'right', energy-saving credentials. But then, in the same month, an article appeared in *The Guardian* (see the next page), which outlined the full extent of CO_2 emissions from shipping. An extract follows the *Beluga* article. These two texts are a good example of the paradoxes we meet at every point when we start thinking about the environment. What difference will the *Beluga* make in a global context? But then again, we have to start somewhere. Of course you can feel a bit self-satisfied if your family buys a more economical car. But in Eastern Europe, China and India, the wealthy love 4x4s[1], so any efforts we make are being cancelled out elsewhere. Bio-fuels are more environmentally friendly than fossil fuels – but food prices are already rising as more land is given over to fuel-producing crops. You can probably think of other examples.

Cargo Ship Sails

A commercial cargo ship, MS *Beluga*, partially powered by a giant kite-sail, departed in February from the port of Bremerhaven, Germany, bound for Venezuela. The computer-controlled kite, measuring 160sq m (1,722sq ft), could cut fuel consumption by as much as 20% as it tugs[2] the ship – helping to reduce carbon dioxide emissions. It is estimated that shipping accounts for 90% of world trade transportation and 4% of global CO_2 – twice the emissions of the airline industry.

---

[1] **4x4s** (large, thirsty) four-wheel-drive vehicles (the term usually refers to larger vehicles than SUVs)   [2] **to tug** to pull along

Activities

1. How does the Beluga save fuel?
2. What advantages and disadvantages of this system can you think of?

Shipping Boom Increases CO$_2$ Emissions

John Vidal

Dirtier than planes, pollution out at sea has been grossly underestimated
When the world's largest merchant ship ferries its monthly cargo of 13,000
containers between China and Europe, it burns nearly 350 tonnes of fuel a
day. The Emma Maersk supplies Britain with everything from toys and
food to clothes and televisions, but its giant diesel engines can emit more 5
than 300,000 tonnes of CO$_2$ a year – equivalent to a medium-sized coal
power station.
Until now, reducing CO$_2$ emissions from the world's fleet of almost 90,000
large ships has not been a priority for governments or shipowners. [...]
The world's burgeoning[1] shipping fleet currently emits 1.21bn tonnes a 10
year, the draft UN report seen by the Guardian says, constituting nearly
4.5 % of world emissions.
Whereas the aviation industry has been at the top of the climate change
agenda, and is expected to be included in the EU's trading scheme, emissions from ships, which emit twice as much CO$_2$ as planes, have gone relat- 15
ively unnoticed.

---

[1] **burgeoning** growing fast (like plants in the spring)

Activities

The facts

1. Make a straightforward list of the main points in the article.

A fair comparison?

2. To what extent is it fair to compare ships with aeroplanes in the
pollution stakes? You should be able to make several relevant points.

3. Why do you think that shipping has escaped the attention of environmentalists until fairly recently, whereas flying has come in for a lot of
criticism?

Islanders Turned Green

David Lister

This text is about the ways in which a small island off the coast of Scotland has managed to find ways to produce all the electricity it needs. How might they have done it?

Kettles will be boiling and toasters popping in a small Scottish island today when its 87 residents receive mains[1] electricity for the first
5 time.

The arrival of electricity from renewables spells the end for Eigg's unreliable and polluting diesel generators

At midday the Isle of Eigg will take a long-awaited step into the modem world when its oldest resident, a 90-year-old woman, flicks a switch[2] in a symbolic ceremony on the pier.

Five wind turbines mean that this tiny Hebridean community off the coast
10 of Skye will become completely self-sufficient thanks to what it claims is a unique combination of wind, hydro-electric and solar energy.

As she prepared for the arrival of "Eiggtricity", Sue Kirk, who runs the island shop, said yesterday: "I've just bought a toaster for the first time. I'm going to avoid going on a mad spending spree[3] but with the weather the
15 way it is it's tempting to get a tumble dryer[4] as well because it's been raining non-stop since Christmas."

Until now most houses in this small island, just six miles long by four miles wide, have got by on limited electricity from unreliable diesel generators that pump out clouds of black smoke. Now they will be able to watch televi-
20 sion or switch the lights on whenever they choose. They will be able to live without fear of the freezer defrosting. The island tearoom will be able to power a dishwasher, while Mrs Kirk will be able to extend opening hours.

"It's a massive achievement," said Mrs Kirk. [...] "The fact that it is all from renewables means that we are going to be seen as a role model for the rest
25 of Britain."

Christine Booth, 66, whose husband is chairman of Eigg Electric, the company set up to run the scheme, said: "It's really difficult explaining to people who aren't on the island what a difference it is going to make. "Householders are going to be allocated[5] five kilowatts and businesses and places
30 like the school 10 kilowatts. It means that you can do your washing and you can do your drying and you can also do your ironing, but not all three at the same time." [...]

---

[1] **mains** Netz(strom)   [2] **to flick a switch** to turn something on (the implication is that it's a very easy thing to do – but with major consequences)   [3] **spending spree** a big, enjoyable shopping trip   [4] **tumble dryer** electric clothes dryer which turns slowly, lifting and dropping the clothes inside it (to tumble – normally to fall in the way that small children fall without really hurting themselves)   [5] **to allocate** to give someone (a share of) something in an official kind of way

The £1.6 million scheme combines wind, hydro-power and solar power, all feeding into an island-wide grid[6] serving 60 residential and business properties. It has been funded ₃₅ through residents' donations[7] and grants from the European Union's regional development programme, the National Lottery and the Highlands and Islands Community Energy Company. Since islanders made history in 1997 by buying Eigg from its absentee landlord[8] in a £1.5 million community buy- ₄₀ out, the electricity issue has topped the agenda. After deciding that a cable under the sea from the mainland was too expensive, the community set about organising its own supply.

───────────

[6] **grid** network of electricity cables   [7] **donation** money given for a good cause   [8] **absentee landlord** someone who owns property of some kind but never or hardly ever visits it

Activities

Let's get technical

1. Write a set of questions, the answers to which would tell someone who hasn't read the text what it is about.

2. Work with a partner to answer the questions and turn them into a summary of the text.

Back on the mainland

3. Why would this solution not be feasible for larger areas?

4. Do you know of a fairly large country which produces nearly all its energy from renewable sources? How do they do it?

It's an emotional issue

5. Imagine you are one of the islanders talking to a visitor. Explain how you feel about the new electricity supply.

6. Comment on the use of direct speech in the article.

7. What kind of people do the islanders seem to be?

No telly tonight!

8. Nearly everyone in the developed world takes a reliable electricity supply for granted. How do you think your family would manage if there was a long-term power cut (or outage, as the Americans say)?

State of Fear

Michael Crichton

Most of the material in this book is based on the assumption that global warming, with all the attendant dangers, is actually taking place. Not everyone would agree, and plenty of people are not prepared to face the consequences. In what ways are the danger signals being ignored?

Crichton's book is a strange mixture of adventure fiction and hard facts and tables taken from scientific journals. He sets out to demonstrate that there are plenty of statistics and phenomena which do not support the idea of global warming.

In the novel, environmental campaigners are so worried that they will not win the case for some Pacific islanders whose islands are (allegedly) sinking into the sea, that they are prepared to go to enormous lengths to create environmental disasters themselves – in order to strengthen their case.

Michael Crichton

Extreme weather?

In the first extract, the 'good guys' are listening to a weather forecast which turns out to be based on a press release. Kenner is an environmental expert, Sanjong is his associate, and Evans is a young, rather naive (at this stage) lawyer.

Sanjong nudged Evans, and handed him a sheet of paper. It was a printout
5 of a press release from the NERF[1] website. Sanjong pointed to the text:
"... Scientists agree there will be trouble ahead: more extreme weather events, like floods and tornadoes and drought, all as a result of global warming."
Evans said, "This guy [the weather man] is just reading a press release?"
"That's how they do it, these days," Kenner said. "They don't even bother to
10 change a phrase here and there. They just read the copy outright. And of course, what he's saying is not true."
"Then what's causing the increase in extreme weather around the world?" Evans said.
"There is no increase in extreme weather."
15 "That's been studied?"
"Repeatedly. The studies show no increase in extreme weather events over the past century. Or in the last fifteen years. [...] If anything, global warming theory predicts *less* extreme weather. "
"So he's just full of shit?"
20 "Right. And so is his press release."
Onscreen the weatherman was saying, "– is becoming so bad, that the latest news is – get this – glaciers on Greenland are melting away and will soon vanish entirely. Those glaciers are three miles thick, folks. That's a lotta ice. A new study estimates sea levels will rise twenty feet or more. So
25 sell that beach property now."
Evans said, "What about that one? It was on the news in LA yesterday."
"I wouldn't call it news," Kenner said. "Scientists at Reading ran computer simulations that suggested that Greenland *might* lose its ice pack in the next thousand years."
30 "Thousand years?" Evans said.
"Might."
Evans pointed to the television. "He didn't say it could happen a thousand years from now."
"Imagine that," Kenner said. "He left that out."

---

[1] **NERF** National Environmental Research Fund (fictional)

Activities

1. Summarise what the weather report says about climate change.

2. How does Kenner react?

3. Go through the extract and pick out statements by Evans which show how his views are becoming more sceptical. Comment briefly on each statement.

4. Explain how the weatherman has distorted the original press release.

5. What do you know about the Greenland ice pack? (See pages 15 – 17)

6. List some aspects of global warming which you have read about or seen discussed on TV. How far was the information convincing?

7. In the light of your previous answer, try to decide whether Kenner is right to be so sceptical.

8. Have a look at the following statistics.
New York and Albany are in the same state. How could the temperature in New York have risen while the temperature in Albany has fallen slightly during the period covered?

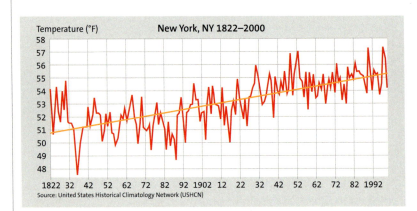

Temperature (°F)   New York, NY 1822–2000
Source: United States Historical Climatology Network (USHCN)

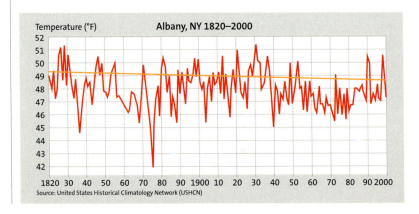

Temperature (°F)   Albany, NY 1820–2000
Source: United States Historical Climatology Network (USHCN)

Extreme environmentalists?

In the second extract, a prominent, wealthy environmentalist, Ann, is asked about her own track record in 'saving the planet'.
The extract begins with a look at the prospects for solar energy.
"[...] But solar panels would work. Silent, efficient ..."
5 "Yes," Kenner said. "And all we need is about twenty-seven thousand square kilometers of panels to do the job. Just cover the state of Massachusetts with solar panels and we'd be done. Of course by 2050 our energy needs will triple, so maybe New York[1] would be a better choice."
"Or Texas. Nobody I know cares about Texas," Ann said.
10 "Well, there you are," Kenner said. "Cover ten percent of Texas, and you're in business. – Although," he added, "Texans would probably prefer to cover Los Angeles first."
"You're making a joke."
"Not at all. Let's settle on Nevada. It's all desert anyway. But I'm curious to
15 hear about your personal experience with alternative energy. What about you yourself, Ann? Have you adopted alternative energy sources?"
"Yes, I have. I have solar heating for my swimming pool. The maid drives a hybrid[2]."
"What do you drive?"
20 "Well, I need a bigger car for the kids."
"How big?"
"Well, I drive an SUV. Sometimes."
"What about your residence? You have solar panels for your electricity?"
"Well, I had consultants come to the house. Only Jerry – my husband – says
25 it's too expensive to install. But I'm working on him."
"And your appliances ...?"
"Every single one is an Energystar[3]. Every one."
"That's good. And how large is your family?"
"Two boys. Seven and nine."
30 "Wonderful. How big is your house?"
"I don't know exactly."
She hesitated.
"Ah hell, tell him, Ann," Bradley[4] said. "She has a *huge* fucking house. Must be ten, fifteen thousand square feet. Absolutely *beautiful*." [...]
35 "And you have a second home?" Kenner asked.
"Shit, she's got *two*," Bradley said. "Got a *fabulous* place in Aspen and a great house in Maine as well." [...]
Kenner said, "How about travel. You use private jets?"
"Well, I mean we don't *own* one, but we catch rides, whatever. We go when
40 people are going anyway. We fill the plane up. Which is a *good* thing."
"Of course," Kenner said. "But I must admit I'm a little confused about the philosophy –" [...]

---

[1] **New York** the state, not the city   [2] **hybrid** economical car which combines petrol and battery power   [3] **Energystar** make of efficient electrical equipment   [4] **Bradley** TV actor who lectures on the environment

Activities

'Saving the planet'?

1. Surely solar energy is a good thing. Try to explain why Kenner seems to be making fun of it.

2. How do Kenner and Ann respectively feel about the choice of areas which could be covered with solar panels?

3. Describe Ann's lifestyle.

4. Why does Ann hesitate (line 32)? Can you find an earlier example of similar behaviour?

5. Discuss Bradley's motives for 'letting the cat out of the bag' about Ann's houses.

6. Explain why Kenner is 'a little confused' about Ann's supposedly 'green' philosophy.

What's his game?

7. Why do you think Crichton has decided to attack the conventional wisdom on global warming?

8. Try to decide what his own position on the environment could be.

9. *State of Fear* was published in 2004. Would it still be credible to write about the environment in this way a few years later?

More strange statistics

10. The conventional wisdom is that rising carbon dioxide levels inevitably result in rising temperatures. *Inevitably?*
    Describe and compare the two graphs. Do you have any theories on the dip in the temperature graph?

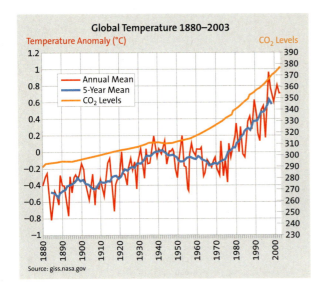

Global Temperature 1880–2003

Source: giss.nasa.gov

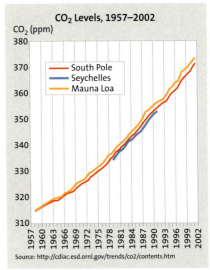

CO_2 Levels, 1957–2002

Source: http://cdiac.esd.ornl.gov/trends/co2/contents.htm

How (Not) to Be Green

Rachel Johnson

Can you point out some of the inconsistencies in the drawing below?   Before you read

Rachel Johnson, the wife and author of the article, speaks first. Her husband works for an environmental agency.

"Darling, do the colleagues that you are enlisting in their thousands in the battle against climate change know that you drive the few hundred yards to
5 the Tube station rather than walk or take the bus?" I said, after I'd been listening for quite some time to him talking to an impressed broadsheet[1] journalist about the importance of recycling grey water.

"Do your colleagues know that you virtually can't get to sleep unless the TV and DVD are left on standby?" I went on, warming to my theme.
10 "And that you don't recycle anything, ever?"

My husband aka[2] Ivo Dawnay [...] laughed uneasily, fielded[3] a call from the Radio 4 Today programme and then lashed out.

"Yes, but you're the one who insisted on having an Aga[4] in London and a Volvo Cross Country," he pointed out, and then I jabbed back about how he
15 never puts a jersey on, and then he retorted that I leave my Blackberry charger on all the time, and I pointed out that he goes to Tesco and returns with cruddy, cheapo "economy" fruit and veg swaddled[5] in packaging and dozens of plastic bags. [...]

---

[1] **broadsheet** 'respectable' newspaper, e. g. *The Times, The Guardian*, cf. 'tabloid' newspapers, e. g. *The Mirror, The Sun*; the words 'broadsheet' (large) and 'tabloid' (small) originally referred to newspaper formats, but some broadsheets (including those mentioned above) appear in semi-tabloid format nowadays   [2] **aka** also known as (a police term as a rule)   [3] **fielded** (here) dealt with appropriately – normally a cricket term, to field the ball means to stop it after the batsman has hit it   [4] **Aga** a type of cooker which enjoys very high social status in Britain; it can be fired by solid fuel or gas/electricity; presumably this model is fired by solid fuel (causing smoke pollution), or the husband could not use his wife's choice of this kind of cooker as an example of her 'non-greenness'   [5] **swaddled** wrapped in several layers; most people associate this word with the baby Jesus wearing what babies wore before there were nappies (*Windeln*)

on scribe

In my experience, there is no other issue in modem times as divisive as the green-living debate.

The greener-than-thou[6] row is all-encompassing, you see. Every decision you make, from eating animals, wearing leather, buying organic[7], holidaying in Britain or abroad, going by car or by train – indeed anything [...] can be very green somewhat green or not green at all. [...]

20

_____

[6] **greener-than-thou** based on a familiar biblical-sounding quotation referring to people who are hypocritical: holier than thou   [7] **organic** *'Bio'*

Activities

Greener than thou?

1. Make a list of the kinds of behaviour and items referred to in the article, and try to decide whether they are 'green', somewhat green or not green at all.

2. For the somewhat green and not green at all items, explain why they could be considered lacking in 'greenness'.

Reading between the lines

3. How do we know that there is a lot of media interest in Mr Dawnay's idea? Why might that be?

4. What evidence is there for saying that the couple featured here are middle-class or above?

Greener than you?

5. Make a personal list similar to the one in activity 2 above, and explain why you still indulge in some activities which are not as green as they might be.

6. Role-play: Work in pairs. One of you pretends to be ultra-green, and the other pretends to be an unreformed character who sees nothing much wrong with flying, thirsty cars, non-organic food, plastic bags for everything and so on. Practise and perform a lively argument.

7. Write a short essay in which you outline your own policy on environmental issues, and also suggest some steps which you think the government should be taking to 'save the planet.'
   Here are some points to think about:
   - There is an English saying which goes: "Look after the pennies and the pounds will look after themselves." How far do you think that this principle also applies to environmental issues? (It would mean that if we in Europe try to do things in an environmentally friendly way at a personal level, we can stop or at least slow down global warming.)
   - Are we actually prepared to take the necessary steps? What would the consequences be for our standard of living? And how about the so-called emerging nations?
   - Do we have any right to try and tell them to save energy (they use far less than we do per person, even if the total amount is very high)? Will it be any good trying to 'set them an example'?

Spiralling towards Destruction

Elizabeth Kolbert

Kolbert's book is widely regarded as one of the clearest, best-researched – and most frightening descriptions of what we are doing to our planet. Think of it as an antidote to the extracts from Crichton's book (pages 44–48). Kolbert claims that in the case of most perceived 'threats' (bird flu or the anti-measles injection, for example), scientists are much less worried than ordinary people, particularly those who read the tabloid newspapers. With global warming it's the other way round. It's the scientists who are really worried. Why might that be?
Here are some of the key points from Kolbert's book.

1. Greenhouse gases

... allow the sun's radiation, which arrives mostly in the form of visible light, to pass freely. But the earth's radiation, which is emitted in the infra-red part of the spectrum, is partially blocked. Greenhouse gases absorb in-frared radiation and then re-emit it – some out toward space and some back
5 toward earth. This process of absorption and re-emission has the effect of limiting the outward flow of energy. As a result, the earth's surface and its lower atmosphere need to be that much warmer before the planet can radi-ate out the necessary 235 watts per square meter. The presence of green-house gases largely accounts for the fact that the average global tempera-
10 ture, instead of zero, is actually a far more comfortable fifty-seven degrees.

2. Scientists at a symposium in Reykjavik

"Let's say that there's three hundred people in this room," (one of the scien-tists told Kolbert). "I don't think you'll find five who would say that global warming is just a natural process."
(Kolbert later went round talking to the scientists, and didn't find a single
5 one who thought global warming was natural.)

3. Species survival – or extinction

Any species that is around today, including our own, has already survived catastrophic climate change. The fact that a species has survived such a change, or even many such changes, is no guarantee, however, that it will survive the next one. Consider, for example, the outsized megafauna – sev-
5 en-hundred-and-fifty-pound saber-toothed cats, elephantine sloths[1], and fifteen-foot-tall mastodons – that once dominated the North American landscape. These megafauna lived through several glacial cycles, but then something changed, and they nearly all died out at the same time, at the beginning of the holocene[2].

---

[1] **sloth** *Faultier*   [2] **holocene** geological period beginning about 10,000 years ago

Over the past two million years, even as the temperature of the earth has 10
swung wildly, it has always remained within certain limits. The planet has
often been colder than today, but rarely warmer, and then only slightly. If
the earth continues to warm at the current rate, then by the end of this
century temperatures will push beyond the "envelope" of natural climate
variability.   15

4. The ice core record

What the Vostok record[3] shows is that the planet is already nearly as warm
as it has been at any point in the last 420,000 years. A possible consequence
of even a four- or five-degree temperature rise on the low end of projections
for this century – is that the world will enter a completely new climate re-
gime, one with which modern humans have no prior experience. When it 5
comes to carbon dioxide, meanwhile, the evidence is even more striking.
The Vostok record demonstrates that, at 378 parts per million, current CO_2
levels are unprecedented in recent geological history.

5. Talking to a politician

Dobriansky[4] began by assuring me that despite how it might appear, the
Bush administration took the issue of climate change "very seriously." She
went on, "Also, let me just add, because in terms of taking it seriously, not
only stating to you that we take it seriously, we have engaged many countries in initiatives and effort, whether they are bilateral initiatives – we have 5
some fourteen bilateral initiatives – and in addition we have put together
some multilateral initiatives. So we view this as a serious issue. [...] The bottom line here is, in grappling with a serious issue, we believe we have a
common goal and objective, but that we can take different approaches."

6. The Chinese angle

Over the next fifteen years, the size of China's economy is expected to more
than double. This projected growth, most of which will be fueled by coal,
overwhelms not just all conservation projects that are currently being un-
dertaken in the United States, but also any that could be reasonably imag-
ined. Hawkins[5] gave me a copy of a presentation he had prepared on future 5
power plant construction. In it was a graph detailing China's plans: by
2010, the country is expected to build 150 new one thousand-megawatt coal
plants (or their generating equivalent); by 2020 it is expected to construct
another 168 new plants. If every single town and city in the United States
were to match the efforts that Burlington[6] has made, the aggregate savings 10

---

[3] **Vostok record** information from a very long ice core drilled at the Vostok station in
Antarctica   [4] **Paula Dobriansky** Under Secretary of State for Democracy and Global Affairs
in the Bush administration (2005)   [5] **Hawkins** David Hawkins, who runs the climate
program for the NRDC (National Resources Defense Council)   [6] **Burlington** small city in
Vermont which set out to reduce energy consumption by 10% from 2002 on, with some
success

would amount – very roughly – to 1.3 billion tons of carbon over the next several decades. Meanwhile, the lifetime emissions just from the new coal plants China is expected to build would amount to some 25 billion tons of carbon. To put this somewhat differently, China's new plants would burn
15 through all of Burlington's savings – past, present, and future – in less than two and a half hours.

7. No need to despair?

China is industrialising according to a model set in the United States forty or fifty years ago: its factories rely on obsolete and highly inefficient motors; its electricity transmission system is antiquated; and although it is the world's primary manufacturer of compact fluorescent bulbs, it barely uses
5 any. (Per unit of gross domestic product, China consumes two and a half times as much energy as the United Sates and nearly nine times as much as Japan.) Were China to bring its factories up to date and fill even a modest amount of its projected energy demand from renewable sources, it is esti- mated that the number of new coal-fired plants it would need to build could
10 be cut by nearly a third.

8. Bye bye homo sapiens?

"Let me[7] just say this. [...] I'm not sure we can solve the problem. I hope we can. I think we have a shot[8]. I mean, it may be that we're not going to solve global warming, the earth is going to become an ecological disaster, and, you know, somebody will visit in a few hundred million years and find
5 there were some intelligent beings who lived here for a while, but they just couldn't handle the transition from being hunter-gatherers to high technol- ogy."

---

[7] the speaker is Marty Hoffert, a professor of physics at New York University   [8] **to have a shot (at something)** to have a try/attempt at sth. with a chance of succeeding

Activities

1. How does the 'good' effect of greenhouse gases work?	1. Greenhouse gases
2. What would life on earth be like without these gases?	
3. And what are the familiar bad effects?	
4. The writer could not find even *one* scientist who thought global warming was a natural process. What does this tell us?	2. Scientists ...
5. What point is the writer making in connection with the "megaspecies"?	3. Species survival ...
6. Why has she made this point?	
7. What is particularly worrying about the present warming process?	

4. The ice core record	**8.** What does the ice core record tell us about temperatures on earth and carbon dioxide levels?
	9. Why should this information worry us?
5. Talking to a politician	**10.** Dobriansky was trying to explain and justify her government's refusal to sign the Kyoto protocol. Did she do a good job? Give reasons for your answer.
	11. How would you describe this kind of talk? Use examples from the extract to support your views.
6. The Chinese angle	**12.** How are the Chinese planning to meet their huge and growing energy demands?
	13. Why is the rest of the world worried?
	14. Do we (in the developed world) have the right to criticise the Chinese? Give reasons for your answer.
	15. Was there any point in Burlington's efforts to save energy (and similar projects elsewhere) in view of what is likely to happen on the energy front in China?
7. No need to despair?	**16.** How could China reduce its energy requirements?
	17. Do you think there is any likelihood of this reduction actually taking place?
	18. What is ironic about China's production of energy-saving lighting?
8. Bye bye homo sapiens?	**19.** When a scientist starts talking like a science fiction author, should we take him seriously or not? Think about the point he is making, and write a paragraph about the future of our species as you see it.
	20. What might survive if we don't?

News flashes

Ask your own questions – and ask your partner to answer them.

The plastic bag menace

Plastic bags are all around us. Blowing down the streets like urban tumbleweed[1], flapping from tree branches, hanging from fences, and every one of them is a symbol of love, the love of a convenience-addicted society for its plastic shopping bags.

Last year Britons used 15 billion of them, or around 250 each. Only one bag in every 200 is recycled in Britain. Apart from the litter problem, they are a menace to wild life.

---

[1] **tumbleweed** dry weed which forms balls and is blown along by the wind

The green land grab

Did you know that charities and some very rich individuals are buying up huge areas of land in lightly-populated areas, claiming they are doing it to protect the environment? For example, US millionaire Douglas Tompkins owns several million acres in Patagonia. Other individu- 5 als and groups own large areas of the Amazon rain forest, coastal areas, wetlands, even quite large areas in densely-populated countries like Britain. They claim they are doing it in order to protect the environment.

But the big recent climate change idea is for rich coun- 10 tries to pay poor ones not to cut down trees in return for carbon credits. Poor countries sell the carbon locked up in their trees to allow rich countries to continue polluting as usual.

1. How do you think the local people feel when they find out that their land has been bought by foreigners or outsiders?

2. Are the new owners likely to treat the land better than the locals?

3. How would carbon credits work? How could the landbuyers benefit?

"Grand Slam"

Here's a man who has received the 'Grand Slam' of international awards: Oscar, Emmy and the Nobel Peace Prize.

1. Who is he, and what do you know about him? (Keep it brief!)

2. What did he do to deserve these awards?

3. You can easily get hold of a DVD of 'his' film – *An Inconvenient Truth* – view it in class or at home, and discuss the message.

4. Is it actually a good film?

Ask your own questions – and ask your partner to answer them.

Porsche threatens legal action

The luxury car make Porsche is likely to take the mayor of London to court over plans to charge drivers of the most polluting vehicles £25 each time they enter the capital. Most high-performance vehicles and 4x4s will have to pay the new higher charge. In the past all vehicles paid 5 the same charge, £8. The extra revenue, estimated at £30m – £50m a year would be ploughed back into environmentally-friendly transport schemes such as walking and cycling. The most environmentally friendly cars will get a 100% discount. 10

1. Could this be the solution to all our energy problems? What problems do you think JAXA will have to overcome?

2. Try to come up with some other radical solutions to our energy problems. What could we do with the world's deserts, for example?

22 years from now

Orbiting solar panels will shoot power to earth using laser beams. The Japan Aerospace Exploration Agency (JAXA) have begun to test ground receiving stations that measure about three kilometers across. (www.thefuture ofthings.com/news/1013/generating-power-in-space. html) ₅

1988 – The Exxon Valdez disaster

- In 1998 the Exxon Valdez spilled 10.8 million gallons of crude oil into Prince William Sound.
- 1,300 miles of coastline were contaminated.
- The oil spill killed 250,000 seabirds, 300 seals, 250 bald eagles and 22 killer whales. ₅
- 26,000 gallons of oil remain in the sandy soil along the coastline.
- The inexperienced third mate was steering the ship when it ran aground. The captain himself, who was not on the bridge at the time, was known to be a lapsed ₁₀ alcoholic.
- Exxon Mobil is dragging its feet over paying 'punitive damages' to the 33,000 fishermen, cannery workers and others who were affected. 6,000 people who were entitled to compensation are already dead. ₁₅
- Only the lawyers have done well out of the disaster.

1. Some elements of this depressing scenario could be considered as 'typical'. Which elements?

2. How likely is a disaster of this kind to occur again?

3. Has anything been done to make disasters of this kind less likely in the future?

4. We would have to say that Chernobyl was an even worse man-made disaster. Why? And how about Hiroshima?

5. Does nuclear energy have a long-term future? What are the arguments for and against?

6. What natural disasters have caused very high levels of death and destruction? Did they also cause widespread pollution?

Examine each of the statements on the right carefully. Try to find out what they mean, and what could be considered the pros and cons in each case.

- "Die deutsche Autoindustrie muss ökologisch werden." (Daniel Goeudevert, former senior manager with Ford Germany and VW)
- Bio-fuels – are they the answer?
- Carbon capture for conventional power stations? 5
- Wind turbines – the perfect source of power?
- Global meltdown as oil runs out?
- There's lots of energy in the sea, isn't there?
- The industrial nations are just too selfish and greedy.
- Never mind the oil running out – the real problems are 10 desertification and food shortages.

And finally …

Will we change our ways in time to save the planet (and our own pleasant life-styles) or is it already too late?

Acknowledgements

Texts   John Wyndham: "The blue planet", from "Meteor" in *The Seeds of Time*,
Penguin, Harmondsworth 1962 (1956), P. 51–52

Kathy Marks: "Indonesia Plants 79 Million Trees", original title: "Ahead of
summit, Indonesia plants 79 million trees to boost its green credentials",
from *The Independent*, 01.12.2007

Midnight Oil: "The Dead Heart", Text: Garrett, Peter Roberts/Moginie,
James Paul/Hirst, Robert George/Rotsey, M./Gifford, P., © by Sprint Music PTY. Ltd., Sony/ATV Music Publishing (Germany GmbH), Berlin

Jim Yardley: "China's Giant Dams", original title: "At China's Giant Dams,
Turbulent Problems Rise Along With the Water", from *The New York Times
(SZ)*, 26.11.2007

Sarah Lyall: "Greenland Goes Green – Again , original title: "Warming Re-
vives the Flora and Fauna of Greenland", from *The New York Times (The
Observer)*, 04.11.2007

Elizabeth Kolbert: "History as Ice-Story", from *Field Notes from a Catastro-
phe: A Frontline Report on Climate Change*, Bloomsbury Publishing, London, 2007 (2006), p. 50–52

Ernest Callenbach: *Ecotopia*, Pluto Press, London, 1978 (1975), p. 17–18

Juliette Jowit: "Saving London", original title: "Price of saving London from
floods could exceed £20bn", from *The Observer*, 10.06.2007

Steve Connor: "Arctic Sea Ice Is Melting – Fast", original title: "Scientists
warn Arctic sea ice is melting at its fastest rate since records began", from
The Independent, 15.08.2007

Elizabeth Kolbert: "Floating Houses", op. cit., p. 131–132

Stanley Kunitz: "The War against the Trees, from John Wain (ed.): *Anthology
of Modern Poetry*, Hutchinson, London, 1963, p. 79–80

Stephen Speight: "Cars, Cars, Cars", original text, 2008

Chris Chilton: "A Car-lover's Lament", original title: "Saving the environment
will be the death of driving pleasure", from *CAR*, February 2008, p. 42

Robin McKie, "Oil Apocalypse", original title: "New 'disaster movie' warns
world of oil apocalypse", from *The Observer*, 04.11.07

Nicholas Crane: "Why We Must Give up Flying", from *Daily Telegraph* (Travel
Section), 29.07.2008

Marillion: "The Last Century for Man", lyrics by Steve Hogarth

N.N.: "Cargo ship sails", from *Practical Boat Owner*, April 2008, p. 9

John Vidal: "Shipping Boom Increases CO_2 Emissions", original title: "True
scale of CO_2 emissions from shipping revealed", from *The Guardian*,
13.02.2008

David Lister: "Islanders Turned Green", original title: "Islanders turned on
by green electricity", from *The Times*, 01.02.2008

Michael Crichton: "Extreme Weather", from *State of Fear*, HarperCollins,
New York 2004, p. 362–363

Michael Crichton: "Extreme Environmentalists", from op. cit., p. 480–481

Rachel Johnson: "How (Not) to Be Green", original title: "A green battle at
home", from *The Sunday Times*, 24.02.2008

Elizabeth Kolbert: "Spiralling Towards Destruction", from op. cit., various pages

Sean Poulter and David Derbyshire: "The plastic bag menace", original title: "Banish the Bags", from *Daily Mail*, 27.02.2008

John Vidal: "The green land grab", original title: "The great green land grab", from *The Guardian*, 13.02.2008

Matthew Taylor: "Porsche threatens legal action", original title: "Porsche threatens legal action on £25 congestion fee", from *The Guardian*, 20.02.2008

N. N.: "22 years from now", from *Daily Telegraph* (Review Section), 16.02.08

Leonard Doyle, "1988 – The Exxon Valdez disaster", original title: "Exxon could face payout 20 years after oil spill", from *The Independent*, 28.02.2008

Illustrations

© NASA/ScienceSource/OKAPIA: p. 4/5; Elke Eberle, Neuhausen: p. 7 top l.; © Bidgee: p. 7 top r.; © picture-alliance/dpa: p. 7 middle, p. 13, p. 25, p. 29 middle, p. 30, p. 42, p. 45, p. 54; © dpa-Fotoreport: p. 7 bottom l.; © OKAPIA: p. 7 bottom r.; A.Rouse / WILDLIFE: p. 8 top; © Michael Nolan/ SplashdownDirect/ Splashdown/images: p. 8 bottom; © Rainer Hackenberg/VISUM: p. 9 top; © digitalstock.com: p. 9 bottom; © REUTERS/Paulo Santos: p. 10; © AP Photo/Dita Alangkara: p. 11; AP Photo/Rick Rycroft: p. 12; © picture-alliance/OKAPIA: p. 17; „Jacket Cover", from ECOTOPIA by Ernest Callenbach. Used by permission of Bantam Books, a division of Random House, Inc.: p. 18 bottom; © Schapowalow/Robert Harding: p. 20; Chris Riddell/Guardian News & Media Ltd 2007: p. 21; © Bildermehr/Hinrich Baesemann: p. 22; Dura Vermeer Groep NV: p. 24; Matthias Berghahn, Bielefeld: p. 27, p. 31, p. 43 bottom, p. 44, p. 49; © Michael Urban/ddp: p. 28 top; © REUTERS/Stringer: p. 28 bottom; © picture-alliance/ZB: p. 29 top; © Wolfgang Horsch: p. 29 bottom; © Paresh Nath: p. 34; © Ken Cox: p. 37; © picture-alliance/jazzarchiv: p. 39; ©2008 SkySails GmbH & Co. KG. All rights reserved.: p. 41; © die bildstelle/ATLAS PHOTOGRAPHY: p. 43; © picture-alliance/Keystone: p. 55 bottom; AP Photo: p. 56; © Jim Wark/Peter Arnold: p. 57; other illustrations: Verlagsarchiv Schöningh